Sing the Alphabet Song! Then color the letters in your name and write it on the line below.

Name:_____

1

MAKING WORDS

Practice tracing the letters with your finger and saying the sentences and sounds of the letters below.
Then write the beginning sound for each word.

Remember: When reading the letters after each sentence, you should say the sound each letter makes, not the letter name.

Say, "Snake, snake, S...S...S," while making a slithery snake motion with your hand.

Say, "Apple, apple, A...A...A," while pretending to eat an apple.

Say, "Tiger, tiger, T...T...T," while making claws with your hands and roaring.

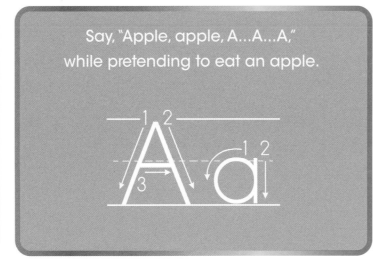

_____ pple

_____ iger

_____ urtle

_____ nake

_____ corn

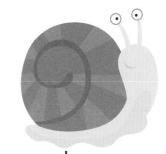

_____ nail

MAKING WORDS

Practice tracing the letters with your finger and saying the sentences and sounds of the letters below.
Then write the beginning sound for each word.

Remember: When reading the letters after each sentence, you should say the sound each letter makes, not the letter name.

Say, "Iguana, iguana, I...I...I," while sticking your tongue out like an iguana.

Say, "Koala, koala, K...K...K," while pretending you're hugging a tree.

Say, "Night, night, N...N...N," while closing your eyes like you're pretending to sleep.

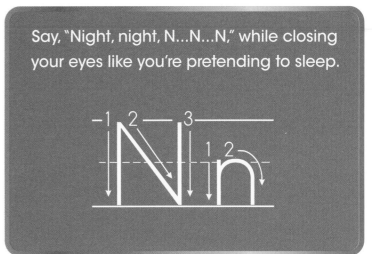

__ ight

__ guana

__ ite

__ sland

__ oala

__ est

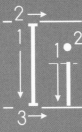

3

MAKING WORDS

Practice tracing the letters with your finger and saying the sentences and sounds of the letters below.
Then write the beginning sound for each word.

Remember: When reading the letters after each sentence, you should say the sound each letter makes, not the letter name.

Say, "Crab, crab, C...C...C," while pretending to make crab claws with your hands.

Say, "Pig, pig, P..P..P," while scrunching your nose up like a pig.

Say, "Eagle, eagle, E...E...E," while bending your arms and flapping them like wings.

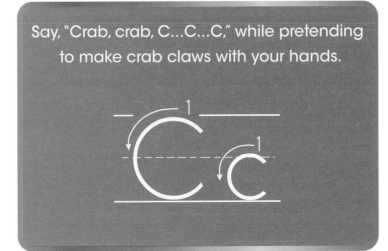
____ a t

____ a g l e

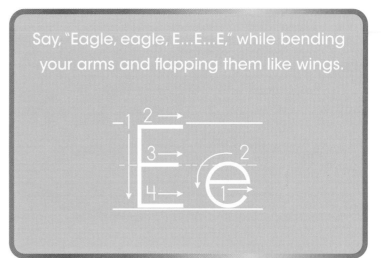
____ i g

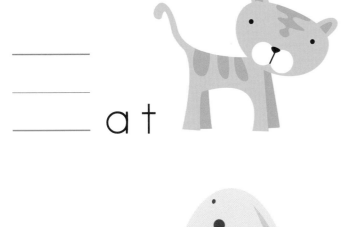
____ g g

____ a i l

____ o a t

SIMPLE SENTENCES

Touch each dot and say the word. Then draw a line from the last word's dot to the matching picture's dot.

I see the bat.

I see the dog.

I see the frog.

I see the hat.

I see the map.

I see the hen.

Write your favorite sentence below.

MAKING WORDS

Practice tracing the letters with your finger and saying the sentences and sounds of the letters below.
Then write the beginning sound for each word.

Remember: When reading the letters after each sentence, you should say the sound each letter makes, not the letter name.

Say, "Hand, hand, H...H...H," while waving your hands high in the air.

Say, "Rabbit, rabbit, R...R...R," while making rabbit ears with your hands.

Say, "Monkey, monkey, M...M...M," while scratching yourself and bouncing around.

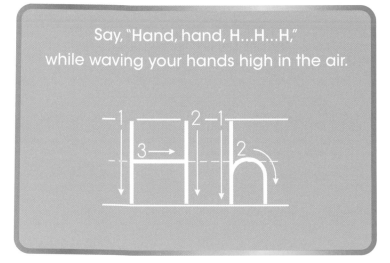  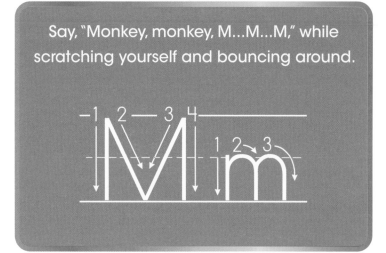

 ___ oon

 ___ eart

 ___ obot

 ___ abbit

 ___ onkey

 ___ orse

MAKING WORDS

Practice tracing the letters with your finger and saying the sentences and sounds of the letters below.
Then write the beginning sound for each word.

Remember: When reading the letters after each sentence, you should say the sound each letter makes, not the letter name.

Say, "Dog, dog, D...D...D," while barking like a dog.

Say, "Garden, garden G...G...G," while pretending to smell flowers you have picked.

Say, "Owl, owl, O...O...O," while flapping your arms like wings.

___ r u m

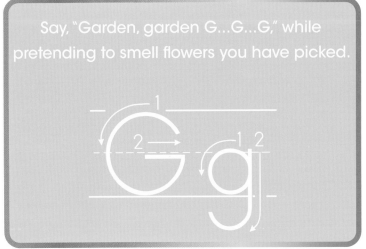

___ w l

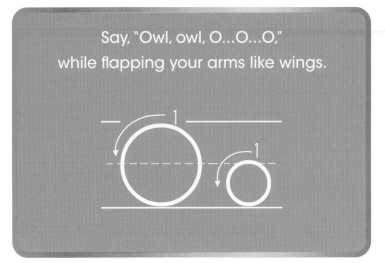

___ o g

___ o a t

___ a r d e n

___ c t o p u s

MAKING WORDS

Practice tracing the letters with your finger and saying the sentences and sounds of the letters below.
Then write the beginning sound for each word.

Remember: When reading the letters after each sentence, you should say the sound each letter makes, not the letter name.

Say, "Lion, lion, L...L...L," while roaring and making your hands look like paws.

Say, "Flower, flower, F...F...F," while opening your fingers like a flower.

Say, "Baby, baby, B...B...B," while pretending you're rocking a baby.

_____ ion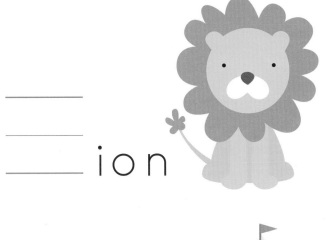

_____ ish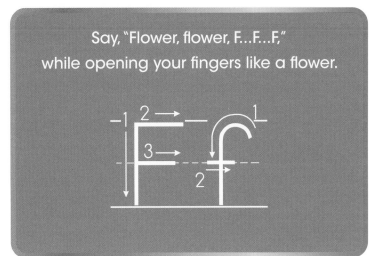

_____ izard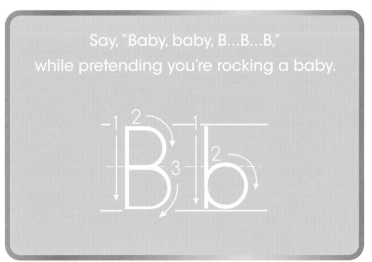

_____ oat

_____ all

_____ lower

SENTENCE SCRAMBLE

This sentence is all mixed up. Draw a line from each picture to the boxes below to put them in the correct order.
Then write the sentence correctly below the puzzle.

hopping. | rabbits | The | are

1	2	3	4

MAKING WORDS

Practice tracing the letters with your finger and saying the sentences and sounds of the letters below.
Then write the beginning sound for each word.

Remember: When reading the letters after each sentence, you should say the sound each letter makes, not the letter name.

Say, "Queen, queen, Q...Q...Q," while pretending to put a crown on your head.

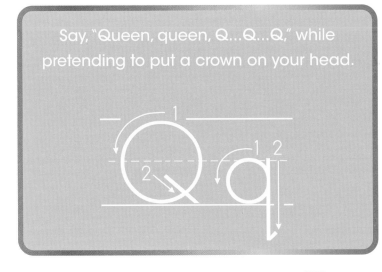

Say, "Unicorn, unicorn, U...U...U," while prancing like a unicorn.

Say, "Jump, jump, J...J...J," while jumping up and down.

_____ mbrella

_____ uice

_____ uail

_____ ueen

_____ ump

_____ nicorn

MAKING WORDS

Practice tracing the letters with your finger and saying the sentences and sounds of the letters below.
Then write the beginning sound for each word.

Remember: When reading the letters after each sentence, you should say the sound each letter makes, not the letter name.

Say, "Zebra, zebra, Z...Z...Z," while galloping like a zebra.

Say, "Worm, worm, W...W...W," while wiggling like a worm.

Say, "Violin, violin, V...V...V," while pretending to play a violin.

____ alrus

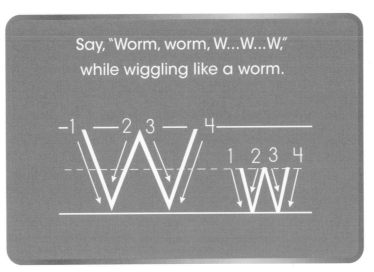

____ an

____ ipper

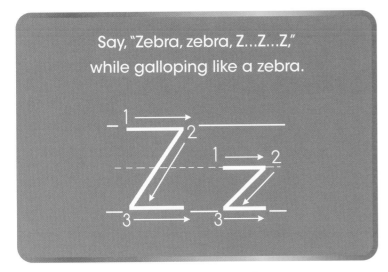

____ ebra

____ agon

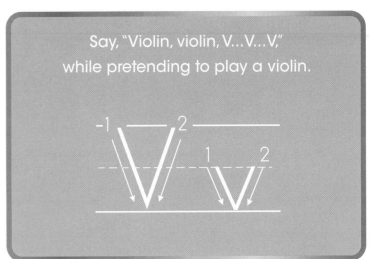

____ iolin

MAKING WORDS

Practice tracing the letters with your finger and saying the sentences and sounds of the letters below.
Then write the beginning sound for each word.

Remember: When reading the letters after each sentence, you should say the sound each letter makes, not the letter name.

Say, "Yo-yo, yo-yo, Y...Y...Y,"
while pretending to play with a yo-yo.

Say, "X-ray, x-ray, X...X...X,"
while pretending to take an x-ray.

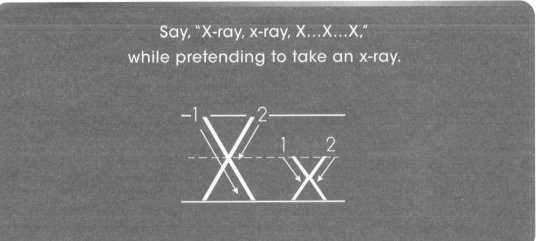

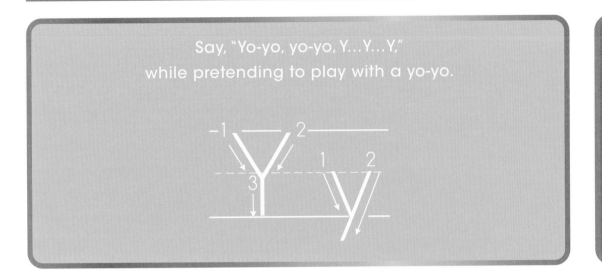

_____ o-yo

_____ ak

fo _____

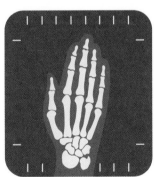

_____ -ray

_____ arn

WHICH WORD?

Say each sound in the words and blend the sounds together.
Circle the correct word below each picture and then color the pictures.

cat   cap   peg   pig   hit   hat   bed   bad

sit   six   dog   dig   fog   frog   bat   bet

jug   jog   beg   bug   her   hen   tan   ten

MAKING WORDS

Sometimes two or more letters together make one sound. Practice tracing the letter combinations with your finger and saying the sentences and sounds of each one.

Remember: When reading the letters after each sentence, you should say the sound the letters make, not the letter names.

Say, "s...h...sh...sh...sh," while putting your finger to your lips.	Say, "t...h...th...th...th," while putting your tongue between your teeth.	Say, "c...h...ch...ch...ch," while flapping your arms like chicken wings.	Say, "w...h...wh...wh...wh," while blowing air out of your mouth.	Say, "i...n...g...ing...ing...ing," while jumping in a circle.

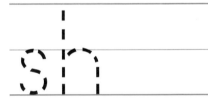 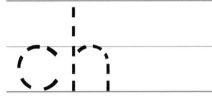 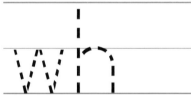  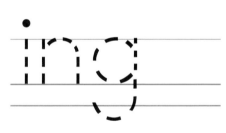

Practice tracing and writing the letter combinations below.

sh   th   ch   wh   ing

Write the missing letter combination for each word.

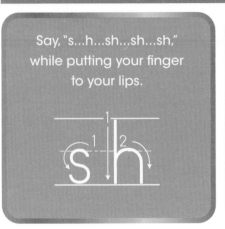 ____ ip

ba ____

____ icken

____ ale

w ____

SUPER SIGHT WORDS

Sight words are words that we see a lot in books and often cannot be sounded out easily.
Practice reading, writing, and spelling these words so you can read them the next time you see them.

a	like	can	said
has	the	I	am

Practice writing the sight words on the lines below.

like _____

can _____

has _____

Complete each sentence using a sight word from above.

_____

I _____ rabbits.

I _____ jump rope.

She _____ a new bike.

SUPER SIGHT WORDS

Read the sight words in the clouds. Then find and circle the sight words in the box.

 he

 is

 me

 she

he	fish	her	go
mom		dog	cap
me	friend	is	she
and	up	she	me
tree	go	her	and
cat	is	funny	car
he	up	bus	cart

up

and

go

her

I CAN WRITE WORDS

Build words with the -at word family and the -ig word family.
Fill in the missing letters to complete the words below. Then color the pictures.

-at or -ig

SIMPLE SENTENCES

Touch each dot and say the word. Then draw a line from the last word's dot to the matching picture's dot.

Look at the pig.
● ● ● ○

Look at the cat.
● ● ● ○

Look at the car.
● ● ● ○

Look at the bed.
● ● ● ○

Look at the bug.
● ● ● ○

Look at the sun.
● ● ● ○

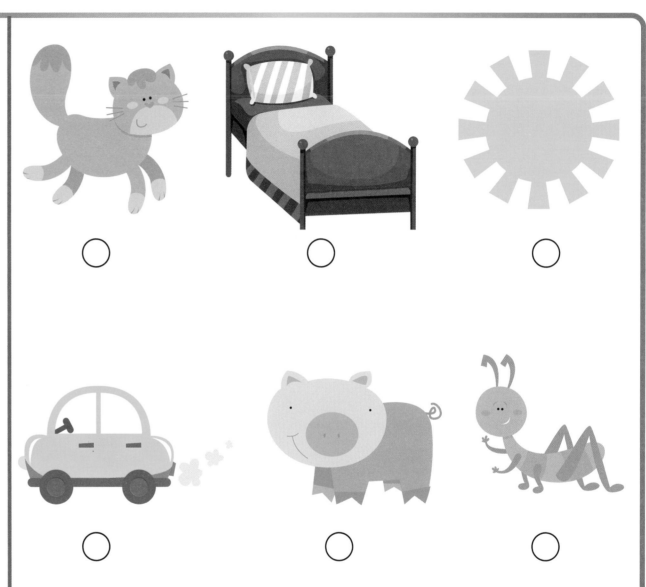

Write your favorite sentence below.

Trace the numbers 1 and 2 and the words one and two with your pencil. Then practice writing the numbers and words.

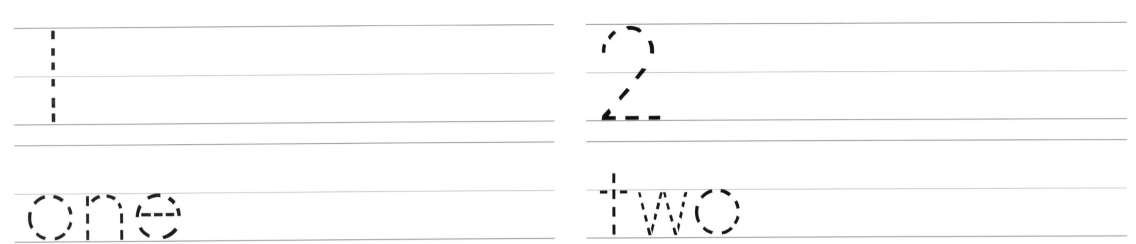

1

2

one

two

Color the three apples red. Count the total number of apples and answer the question. Then color the picture.

How many apples are on the tree? _____

Trace the numbers 3 and 4 and the words three and four with your pencil. Then practice writing the numbers and words.

Someone forgot the birthday candles!
Draw three candles on top of the birthday cake.

Where are the pizza toppings?
Draw four of your favorite toppings on the pizza.

KNOW YOUR NUMBERS

Help Max catch bugs for his collection. Circle the sets of three bugs for Max to catch with his net. Then color all of the bugs in the picture.

How many bugs did Max catch with his net? _____

KNOW YOUR NUMBERS

Trace the numbers 5 and 6 and the words five and six with your pencil. Then practice writing the numbers and words.

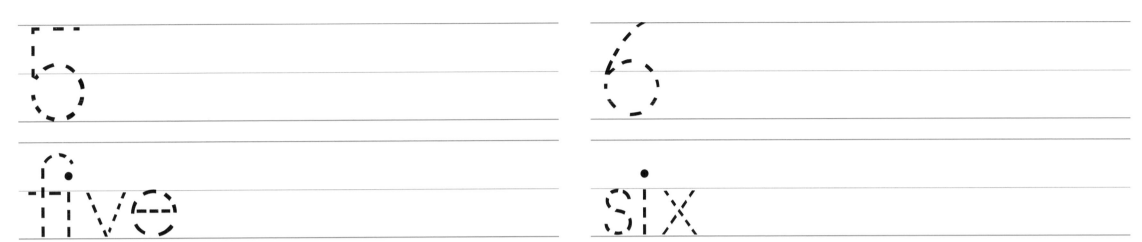

5

6

five

six

Count and color the frogs in the pond. How many frogs are there? _____

Count and color the flowers beside the pond. How many flowers are there? _____

KNOW YOUR NUMBERS

Trace the numbers 7 and 8 and the words seven and eight with your pencil. Then practice writing the numbers and words.

7

8

seven

eight

Help Julie collect shells. Color the sets of seven shells purple and the sets of eight shells yellow. Draw lines to the correct pails where she will put each group of shells to add to her seashell collection.

7

8

AWESOME ADDITION

Draw spots on each butterfly's wings to match the numbers in each equation.
Count the dots on both wings and add them together. Write the sums on the lines.

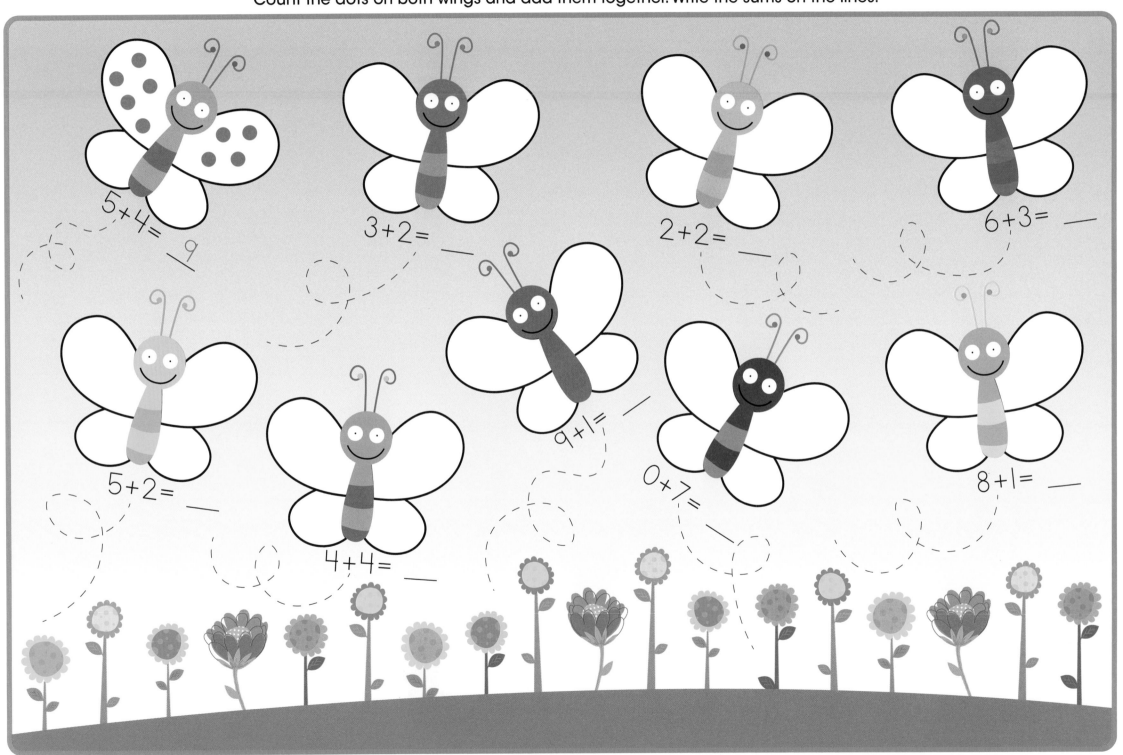

5 + 4 = 9

3 + 2 = ___

2 + 2 = ___

6 + 3 = ___

5 + 2 = ___

4 + 4 = ___

9 + 1 = ___

0 + 7 = ___

8 + 1 = ___

24

KNOW YOUR NUMBERS

Trace the numbers 9 and 10 and the words nine and ten with your pencil. Then practice writing the numbers and words.

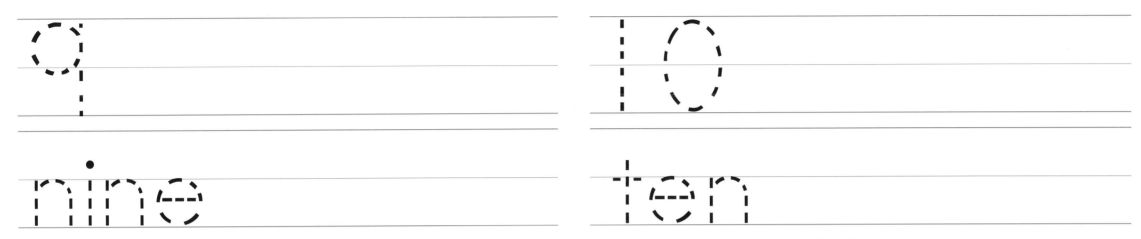

Draw a line from the sets of circus objects to the matching numbers on the signs.

CRAZY COUNTING

Count the objects in each box and circle the correct number.

11   12   13   14   15

11   12   13   14   15

11   12   13   14   15

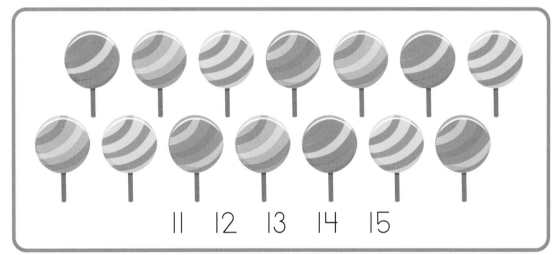

11   12   13   14   15

11   12   13   14   15

Count the objects in each box and circle the correct number.

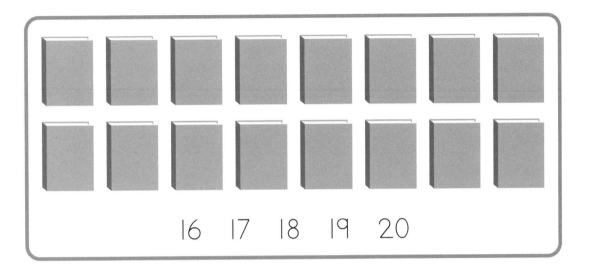

16 17 18 19 20

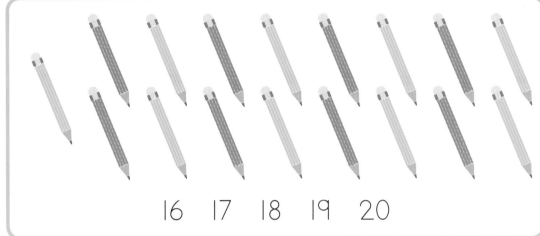

16 17 18 19 20

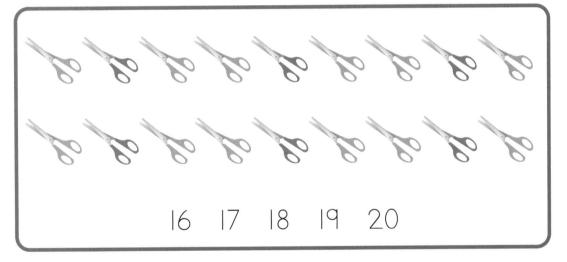

16 17 18 19 20

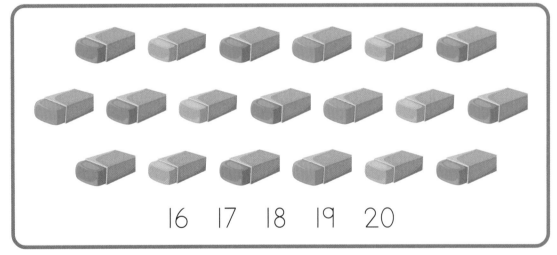

16 17 18 19 20

16 17 18 19 20

FLOWER POWER

Count the petals on each flower. Color the flower with more petals in each box.

Count the flowers in each vase. Circle the vase with fewer flowers in each box.

COLOR COUNTING

Color each set of dots in each section of the picture below based on the color code.

1 dot –   2 dots –   3 dots –   4 dots –   5 dots –   6 dots =

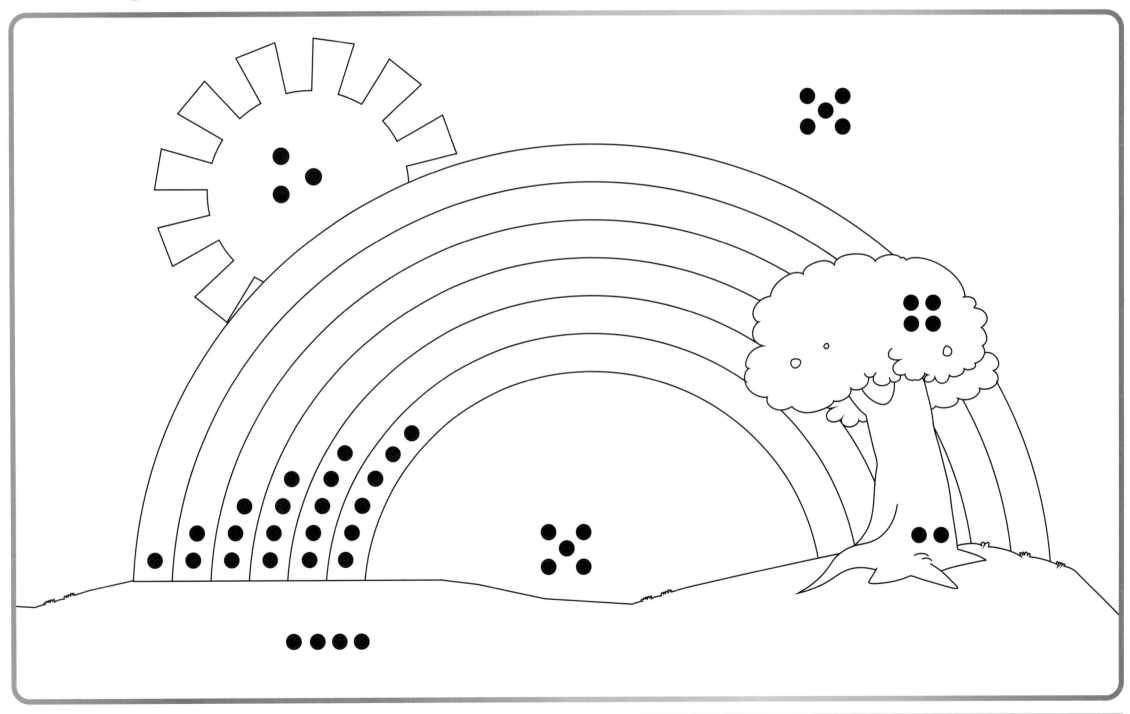

1·2·3 math

Oh no! Ants are at our picnic! Add the numbers on each ant and write the sum for each equation.

2+3 =

4+2 =

5+1 =

3+4 =

3+3 =

4+5 =

5+3 =

5+6 =

BEFORE AND AFTER

Spring has sprung! It is time to water the flowers. Write the numbers that come before and after the number on each watering can in the boxes below.

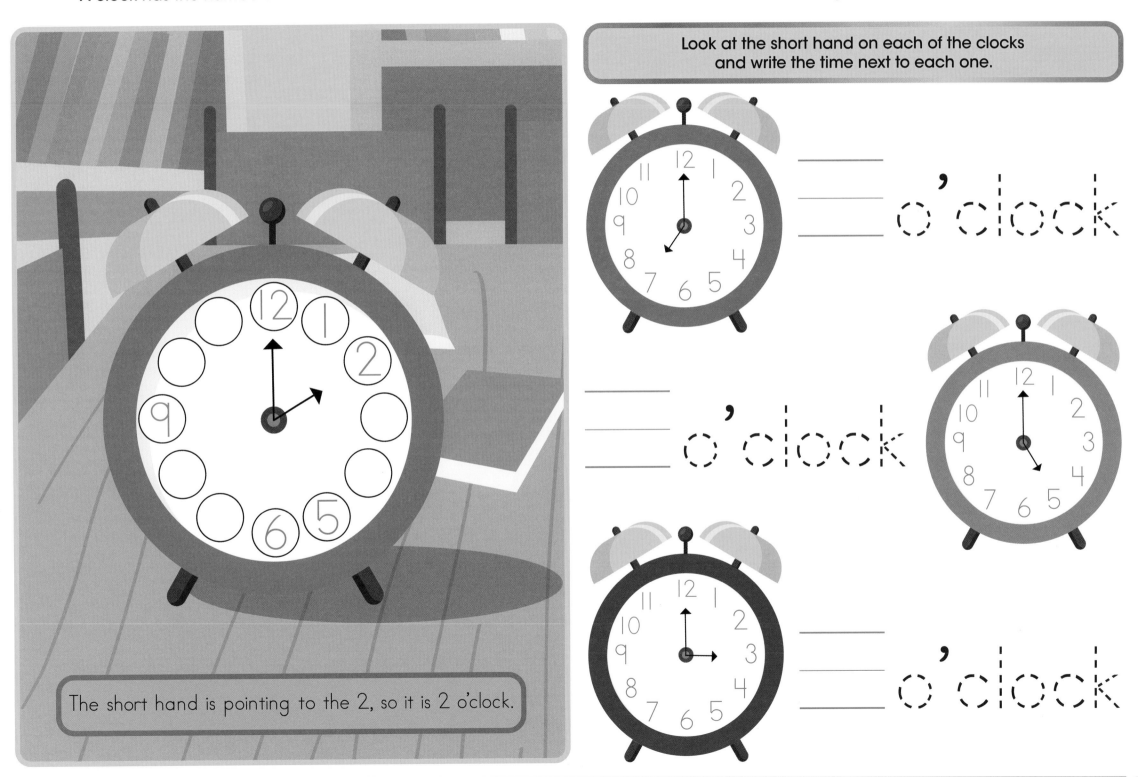

A clock has the numbers 1 to 12 on its face. Look at the clock on the left. Some numbers are missing! Fill in the missing numbers.

Look at the short hand on each of the clocks and write the time next to each one.

_____ o'clock

_____ o'clock

_____ o'clock

The short hand is pointing to the 2, so it is 2 o'clock.

LETTER PRACTICE

Trace the uppercase and lowercase letters with your finger. Then practice tracing and writing them below.

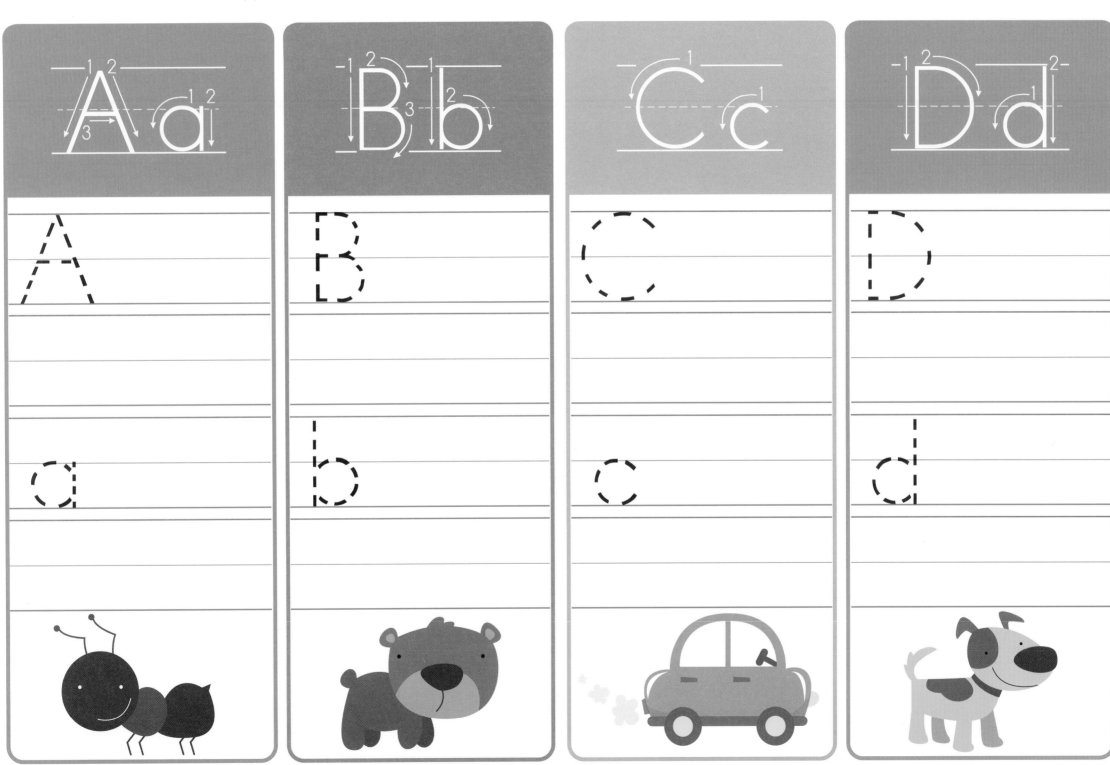

LETTER PRACTICE

Trace the uppercase and lowercase letters with your finger. Then practice tracing and writing them below.

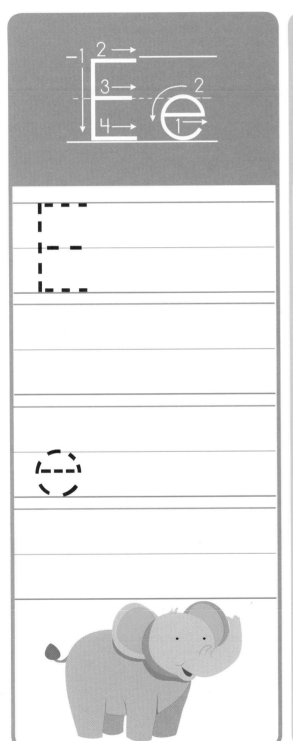

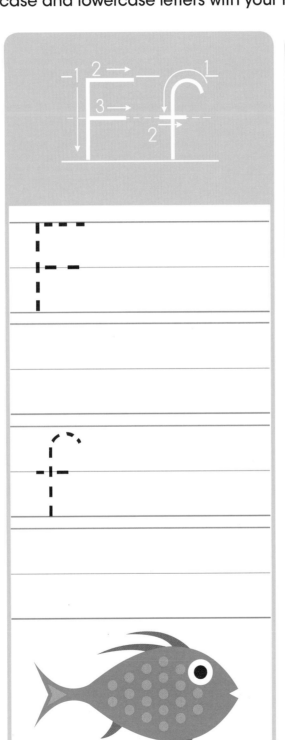

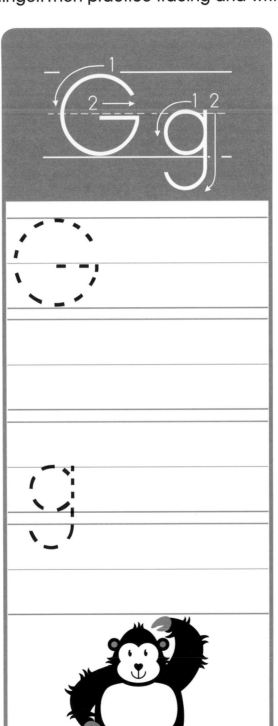

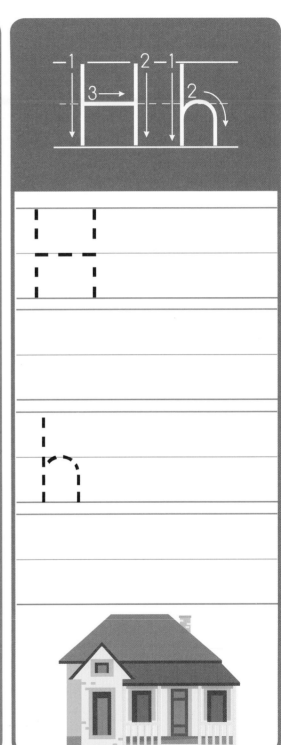

I CAN WRITE WORDS

Build words with the -et word family and the -ug word family.
Fill in the missing letters to complete the words below. Then color the pictures.

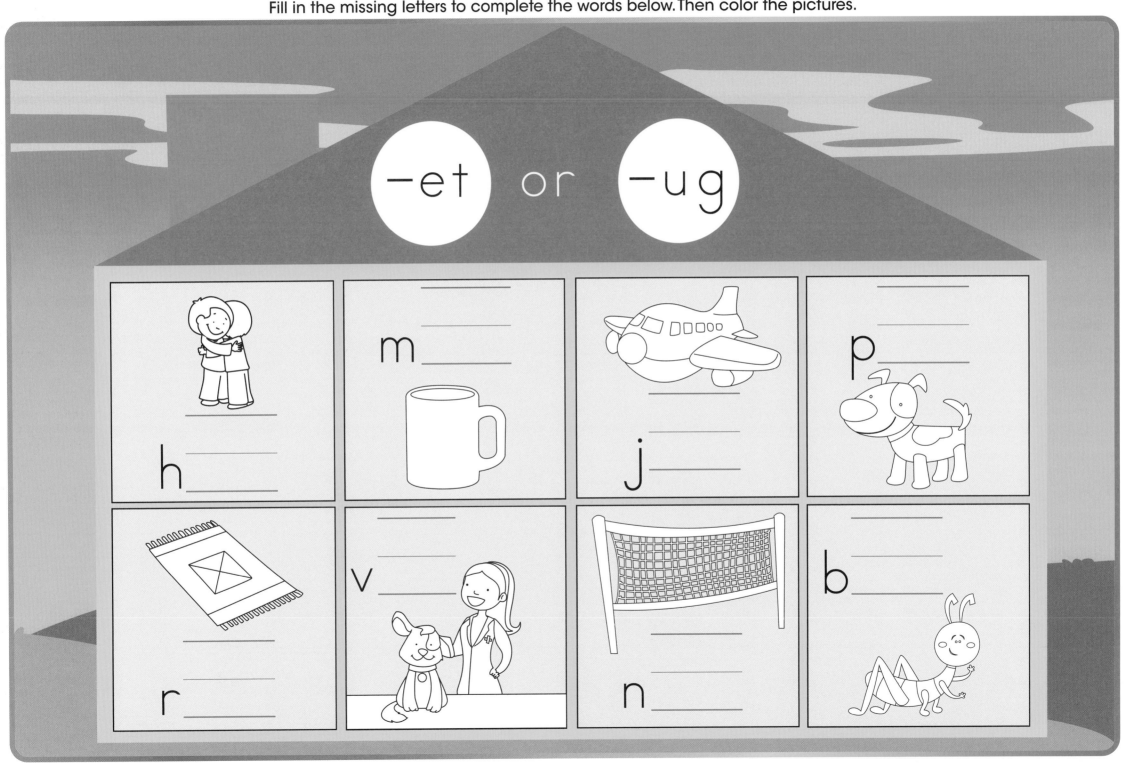

-et or -ug

LETTER PRACTICE

Trace the uppercase and lowercase letters with your finger. Then practice tracing and writing them below.

LETTER PRACTICE

Trace the uppercase and lowercase letters with your finger. Then practice tracing and writing them below.

Silly Sally forgot some important parts of her sentences! She forgot to start with a capital letter and end with a period. Look at the sentences below and rewrite them to fix Sally's mistakes.

i like to play at the park

_____

_____

i have new shoes

_____

_____

you are my friend

_____

_____

i have a pet frog

_____

_____

LETTER PRACTICE

Trace the uppercase and lowercase letters with your finger. Then practice tracing and writing them below.

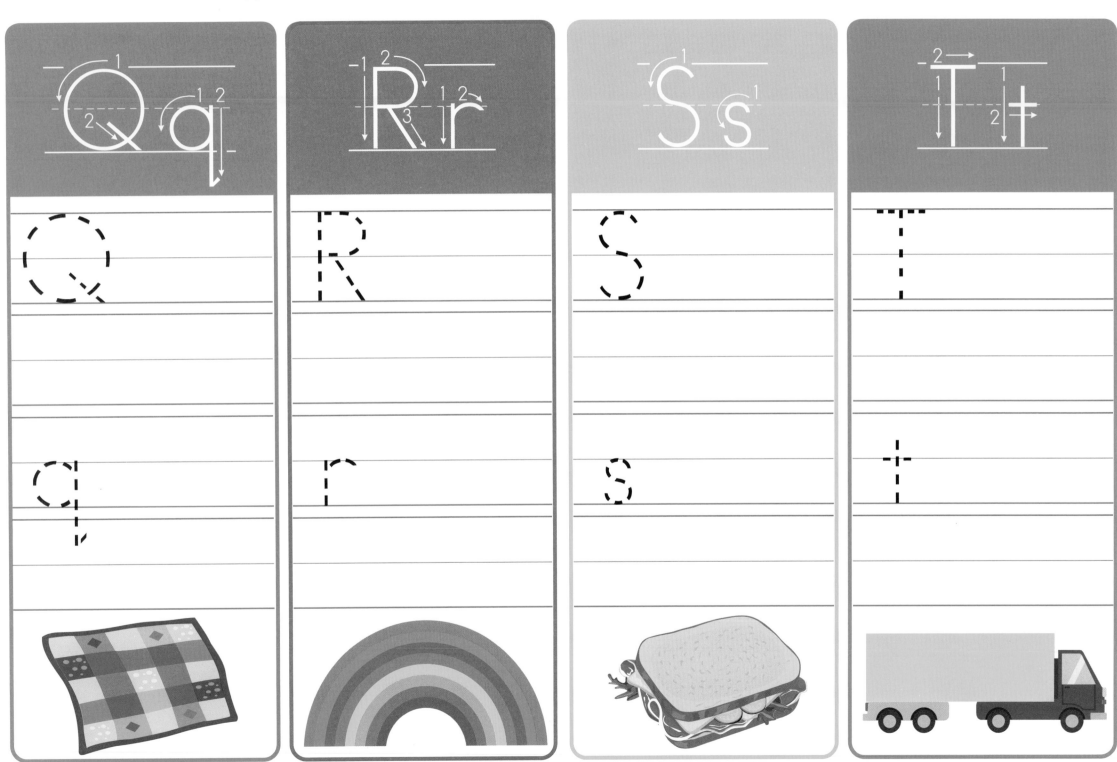

LETTER PRACTICE

Trace the uppercase and lowercase letters with your finger. Then practice tracing and writing them below.

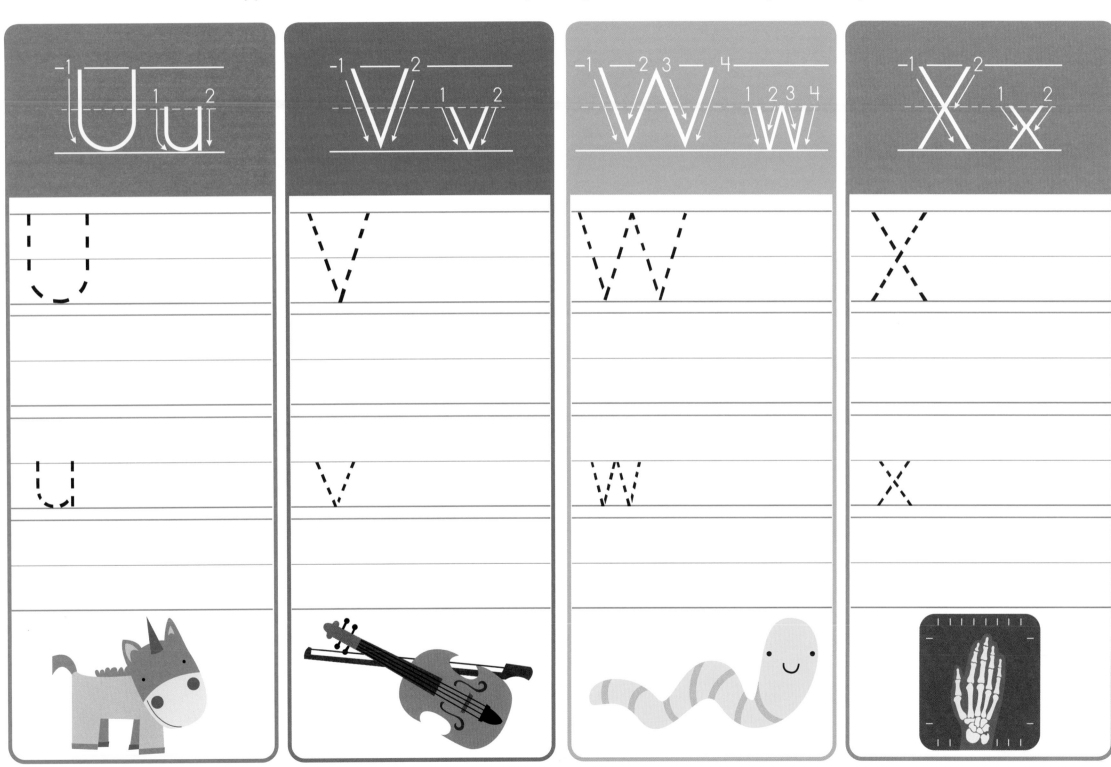

SIMPLE SENTENCES

Touch each dot and say the word. Then draw a line from the last word's dot to the matching picture's dot.

I like the lion.

I like the bear.

I like the rain.

I like the horn.

I like the ship.

I like the drum.

Write your favorite sentence below.

LETTER PRACTICE

Trace the uppercase and lowercase letters with your finger. Then practice tracing and writing them below.

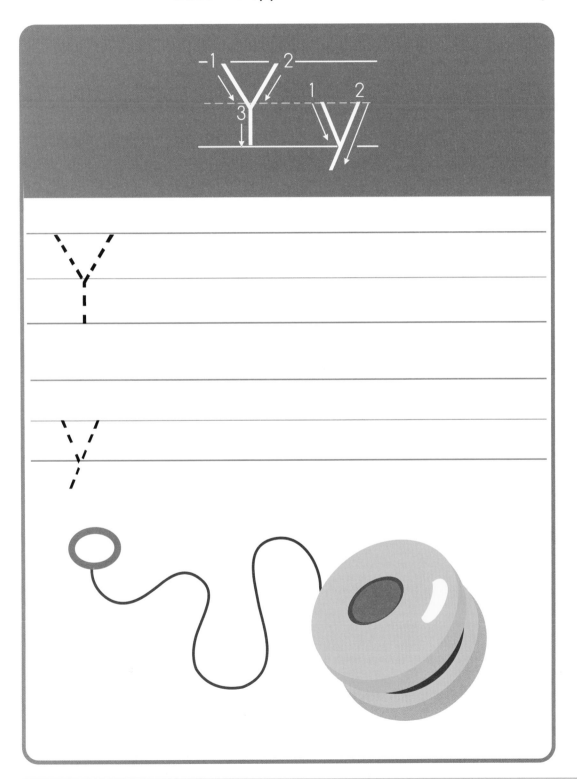

SIMPLE SENTENCES

Touch each word in the box and read it out loud. Complete the sentences below using the words. Then color the pictures.

big	dog	cat	hop

This is a __ __ __ fish.

Hear the __ __ __ purr.

I can __ __ __ on one foot.

I have a cute __ __ __.

Write a sentence below using one of the words from the box above.
Draw a picture to match it.

_____

_____

I AM A WRITER

Writers like to write about their favorite people, animals, places, and things. Write about your favorite animal or place on the lines below.

_____

_____

_____

_____

_____

_____

_____

_____

Draw a picture of your favorite animal or place that you wrote about above.

I AM A WRITER

Writers write about what they think. Remember to use the word because to link what you like to your reason for liking it. Write your opinion about what you like better on the lines below.

OR

_____

_____

_____

_____

_____

Draw a picture of something you like to do.

PRACTICE PAD

Practice writing the alphabet by tracing the uppercase and lowercase letters.

Page 9

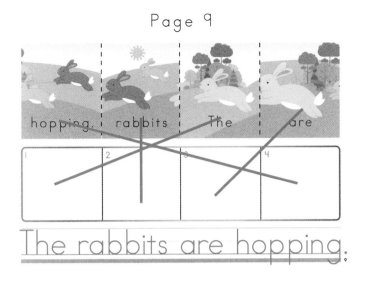

The rabbits are hopping.

Page 13

Page 14

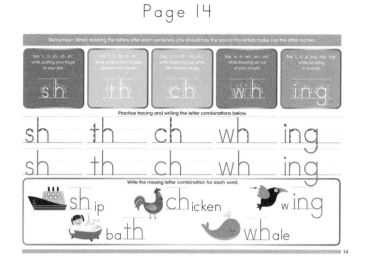

Page 15

Page 17

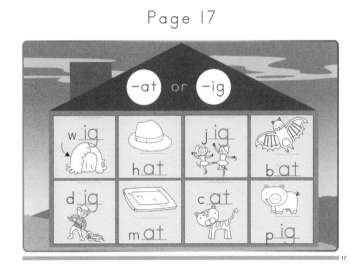

Page 19

Page 21

Page 22

Page 23

Page 24

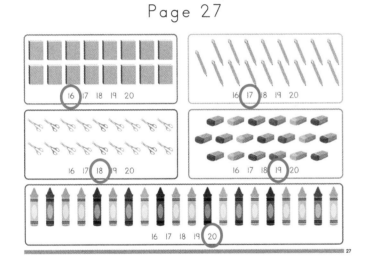

5+4 = 9
3+2 = 5
2+2 = 4
6+3 = 9
5+2 = 7
3+1 = 10
0+7 = 7
8+1 = 9
4+4 = 8

Page 25

q q q q 10 10 10

nine nine ten ten ten

Draw a line from the sets of circus objects to the matching numbers on the signs.

9   10

Page 26

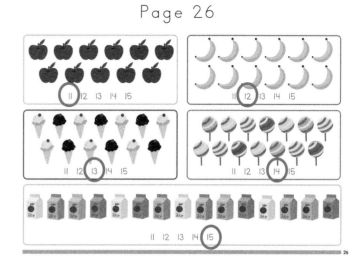

11 (12) 13 14 15
11 12 13 14 15 — (12)
11 12 (13) 14 15
11 12 13 (14) 15
11 12 13 14 (15)

Page 27

(16) 17 18 19 20
16 (17) 18 19 20
16 17 (18) 19 20
16 17 18 (19) 20
16 17 18 19 (20)

Page 28

Count the flowers in each vase. Circle the vase with fewer flowers in each box.

Page 30

2+3 = 5
4+2 = 6
4+5 = 9
5+1 = 6
3+3 = 6
5+3 = 8
5+6 = 11
3+4 = 7

Page 32

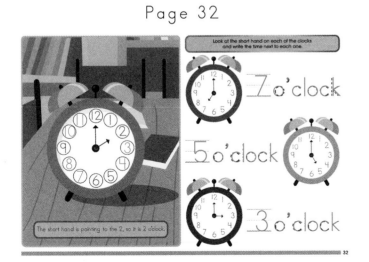

Look at the short hand on each of the clocks and write the time next to each one.

2 o'clock
5 o'clock
3 o'clock

The short hand is pointing to the 2, so it is 2 o'clock.

Page 35

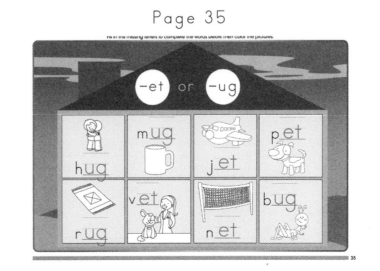

Fill in the missing letters to complete the words below. Then color the pictures.

-et or -ug

mug   p et
h ug   j et
rug   n et   bug   v et

Page 43

big   dog   cat   hop

This is a b i g fish.
Hear the c a t purr.
I can h o p on one foot.
I have a cute d o g.

Write a sentence below using one of the words from the box above.
Draw a picture to match it.